MW00944380

Champion Reading

Speed & Comprehension

Speed Reading for Champions
Volume 1

Written by Jennifer Wozny

ISBN: 978-1-502-41692-6

Table of Contents

CHAPTER 1: Introduction

Welcome to the Champion Reading Course. Champion Reading is a reading enhancement course which provides immediate and measurable results. You are going to learn how to read faster with better concentration, comprehension, and retention. You will also learn how to use mind maps to remember, more efficiently and effectively, what you have read.

This book has been written to introduce speed reading to you in an easy and non-technical way, so that you can learn this highly valuable life-skill.

Power Learning was started in 1983 by Jennifer Wozny in Houston, Texas, U.S.A. The course she developed, Champion Reading, was formerly known as Power Reading, but the name was changed to more adequately reflect what the course was achieving for Mrs. Wozny's students. Students became champion readers and learners. Champion Reading is the vision of Jennifer Wozny. Students were reporting that grades increased, self-esteem was soaring, and that previously poor results on timed tests, due to not being able to finish in the allotted time span, were a thing of the past!

She began the company because she felt that generic speed reading was not delivering what students actually needed to succeed. Amid the throes of rearing her three children during their school and college careers, she also gained insight into the skills students were not being taught for immediate and lasting academic success.

After lots of trial and error, research and years of experience, we can now offer the basics of this most excellent reading enhancement course. This volume is the culmination of many years of teaching thousands of students this constantly evolving skill. Jennifer is a native of London, England, receiving her education there before coming to the United States in 1969. This course has been taught successfully at public and private schools, universities, corporations, and to individuals at the Power Learning Centers in Houston, Texas.

Power Learning has been teaching the Champion Reading course (formerly known as Power Reading) in the Houston, Texas area since the 1980's. Further on in this book there are three lessons with detailed instructions that will enable you to get the foundation of this valuable skill.

CHAPTER 2: Background

Let me introduce you to a true Renaissance man. He was Desiderius Erasmus and he was born on October 28, 1466 and died on July 12, 1536. He was a Dutch scholar and the greatest classicist in northern Europe.   The reason I introduce him is that he was the ***last known human to read everything written in his day***.   After this period of time the volume of information written on every single subject simply exploded. (The printing press was invented by Mr. Gutenberg in 1450.)   This was the beginning of the information explosion.

A person today would be hard pressed to read everything written on any one subject.   We are bombarded with information constantly via our computer, cell phones, as well as the ever-expanding social media streams of data. It is easy to understand why so many students and adults feel totally overwhelmed with their required reading.

Speed reading was first developed by Mrs. Evelyn Wood when she was a student in 1945 at the University of Utah. She observed one of her professors reading very rapidly with excellent comprehension, and then was intrigued to discover that some people could do this naturally.

Some of the most famous people who were naturally fast and proficient readers were H.L. Mencken who could read a 250 page book in an hour, President Theodore Roosevelt who was known to read three books a day while serving as President, and President John F. Kennedy who was also known as a prolific reader.

Mrs. Wood went on to create a very successful speed reading method which was taught worldwide.

What we wish to accomplish is to teach you the skills of speed reading with intense concentration, comprehension and retention. If you wish to read faster just follow the instructions, starting with Lesson 1. Use your own novel, and continue through the course.

The lessons contained in this volume are suitable for children from a 5th grade reading level, and are highly beneficial for students attending junior high, high school, college, as well as adults.

You will be able to transition naturally to textbooks and technical reading once you have mastered this Basic Course and completed the Advanced Course. At that time you will achieve a speed which allows you to filter out extraneous distractions.

The ability to read faster, with greater comprehension and retention, creates a competitive edge that is an essential key to becoming highly effective and more successful. Once you master the basic techniques contained in the three easy lessons in this volume, success will be within reach. You will experience positive results almost immediately.

Champion Reading is a combination of some of the original methods as well as the experience gained since 1983 while teaching thousands of students of all ages and abilities. This was achieved by adding to, subtracting, modifying and adjusting the original methods to more adequately address the needs of students and business professionals in the 21st century.

CHAPTER 3: How does it work?

The process awareness approach uses a natural method with no machines, complex devices, or a multitude of equipment. In fact, all you will need to master this skill are:

- A book (a novel is best)
- Three paper clips (or sticky flags)
- A timer
- Calculator
- Paper
- Pen or pencil

This method is intense, productive and enjoyable. The emphasis is on concentration, and "working smarter rather than harder". The ability to deal with today's information explosion is greatly expanded through:

Increased

- Reading speed
- Reading comprehension
- Ability to concentrate
- Retention
- Confidence

Eliminating

- The dread of reading

Champion Reading course content includes:

- Pacing
- Multiple reading procedures
- Mind map system
- Purpose
- Flexibility

Champion Reading Learning process provides:

- Active learning vs. passive learning
- Written instructions
- Diagrams
- Drills/practice
- Explanation of theory
- An advanced version of this volume to further your skills.

Champion Reading results in:

- Improved reading and comprehension
- Increased understanding, information and retained knowledge
- Thought provoking ideas and creativity
- Organized thought patterns
- Organized system for recall
- Improved understanding of figurative and connotative meanings.
- Increased vocabulary because you (hopefully) will read more.

CHAPTER 4: Mission

"You tell me, and I forget. You teach me, and I remember. You involve me, and I learn."
              -- Benjamin Franklin

The mission of Power Learning is to increase an individual's lifetime capacity for retaining and utilizing knowledge, positively influencing the success and achievement of personal goals, by providing improved reading, learning and vocabulary skills.

We seek to increase awareness that reading efficiently is a skill of lifetime importance. Mastering this new skill will improve reading abilities and information processing.

CHAPTER 5: Goals

The goals of this book are:

- To increase awareness that reading efficiently is a skill of lifetime importance

- To participate actively in improving the education process for middle school, high school and college students

- To provide continuing education for professionals and others in the work force

- To enable you to deal with printed materials more rapidly and effectively

- To enable you to process information based on individual learning styles, and updated teaching methodology

- To enable you to become more productive and better informed, giving you a "competitive edge" for the twenty-first century

- To enable you to become information- targeted.

CHAPTER 6: The Process

The Champion Reading course employs methods of instruction that encompass all learning styles:

KINESTHETIC learners benefit from using their hand as a pacer while reading.

VISUAL learners are helped through our use of mind maps which aid memory recall and retention.

AUDITORY learners benefit from oral feedback.

Everything you read will become easier, your concentration will become more acute, plus your comprehension and recall will improve.

Active learning vs. passive learning

- Drills/practice
- Visual aids
- Reading materials
- Pacing
- Multiple reading procedures
- Mind map systems
- Purpose
- Flexibility

RESULTS

- Improved speed and comprehension
- Read for information
- Ideas
- Thought patterns
- Organized system for recall
- Meaning understood

CHAPTER 7: What are the Benefits?

- Learn to deal with printed materials rapidly and effectively
- Process information based on an individual's learning style
- Compete more effectively in the marketplace due to increased productivity
- Become information targeted
- Increase your capacity for knowledge – no one's head has ever exploded because it was too full of information!
- Flexibility is possible because you can speed up for pleasure or familiar reading, or slow down for more complex information.

Reading is thinking with an aid. The aid is the printed page containing symbols which act as stimuli for the mind. These symobls trigger the mind to think along specific lines.

To improve your reading you must sharpen your thinking. Learning to read generally down the page is mentally challenging. It involves learning and using new patterns of perceiving. The Champion Reading method requires that you always use your hand to pace yourself.

You will be trained to move down the page, seeing the entire page, all of the words. There is no skimming, skipping, or key word reading.

You will learn to get above the print and view it as if you were in an airplane viewing it from above. As you move down the page, you will eventually see whole areas of print.

You will look for total concepts as well as become aware of details, so that you are reading with intense concentration.

You will not see individual words or phrases, but all the words, in groups.

You will learn to allow all the words to come into your brain rapidly. You do not have time to stop and consider each word individually, to color the meaning with bias or boredom. With Champion Reading the words come in so quickly and intensely that you will not have time to evaluate them until they have become part of the whole idea.

You will become involved with feeling, atmosphere, mood, and will become more a part of the story, thinking with the author. You will receive more vivid and enduring impressions.

You will always use your hand; you will be relaxed, but read alertly. You will become a visual, rather than a vocal, reader.

CHAPTER 8: Good Reasons to Master This Skill

Reading is the key to all knowledge

- You run out of time when taking standardized tests
- Need more time to check answers before conclusion of the test
- Your scores are too low on critical reading exams
- Make mistakes on tests that could be avoided if you had more time
- Misreading directions, therefore not answering the question asked
- Daydreaming while reading
- Falling asleep while reading
- You have to keep going back over material and re-reading
- Dreading reading
- You forget everything you read by the end of the page
- Hate reading
- Losing your concentration while reading
- Unable to remember what you have read
- Constantly behind with assigned reading
- Feeling overwhelmed with volume of reading
- Unable to take tests because of anxiety
- Spending too much time on homework
- You cannot understand your teachers/professors so need to read textbooks
- Difficulty learning in noisy environments
- Easily distracted
- Constantly bringing work-related reading home to stay current
- Trying to balance work and a degree program
- Taking too many notes

- Reluctance to embark on a new degree program because of current reading skill
- You want to learn more for your own development
- You have to be certified in a skill to get a job
- You have to complete a certification program to keep your job
- You feel you just read too slowly
- There are ten books you never finished
- You're lazy and just want to get your reading done faster
- Best reason: it is totally cool to read a book or two a day!

A sad fact of life is that the half life of knowledge is 10 years. That means that 50% of what you learn today is obsolete in 10 years, and 70% is obsolete in 7 years. 90% is obsolete in 10 years. (Standard measurement of meaning). If you are in a high-technology field then the half life of knowledge can be measured in weeks!

Reading well is an art.

This book will teach you the basic rudimentary skills of speed reading, thereby increasing your speed, demonstrate mind mapping which aids your recall, as well as strategies to increase your concentration.

This course has been taught to thousands of people since the 1980's, and their ages range from 10 years to 73. The fastest speed some of our students have achieved was 20,000 words per minute with 100 percent comprehension on a test. The majority of students taking the course in our classes reach average speeds of between 800 to 2500 words per minute with 100% comprehension on a test. The best academic results for some of our students have been perfect scores on the Critical Reading section of the SAT, as well as dramatic increases on the ACT, MCAT, LSAT, GRE, ISEE, etc.

What is the secret? It is very simple. We have a theory that if we can increase the concentration of a student, they can be taught anything, if they so desire. One cannot force desire, merely provide an opportunity for change. If reading is made easier, and note taking and test taking is less stressful, then the student usually finds reading more enjoyable and less taxing.

In this introductory book you will be able to compute your beginning speed, learn how to increase your speed, as well as learn basic mind mapping. There are no tests for comprehension due to the very varied audience this volume is geared toward. In the forthcoming volume on advanced skills there will be comprehension tests suitable for high school level and adult students.

You will need a desire to master this new skill, excel in your studies, and/or become more productive for the Champion Reading course to be successful for you.

Sadly, only sixty percent of the books checked out of libraries get read. The average American television viewer watches 1,800 hours of television per year (average of 6 hours per day). Twelve percent of the population reads 80% of the books published, and the average bestseller usually only has a printing of 300,000 copies. We have had adult clients who have never read an entire book in their lives! (Glad to report we were able to change that sad state of affairs).

High speed is an aid to intense concentration, so if you learn how to intensify your concentration, you will comprehend what you are reading. But, this is not enough. You have to remember what you have read so that you can recall information when you need it. Learning mind mapping will sharpen your concentration, comprehension and definitely aid your recall and long-term retention.

If you follow the lessons presented later in this book, push yourself to practice, and stay focused, you too can be a more effective and thorough reader.

Nothing is impossible, because "impossible" is just an opinion.

We strongly believe in self fulfilling prophesies – try running a "success movie" in your head wherein you master this skill and then become eager to master the advanced techniques in the next book from Power Learning.

If you think you can, you probably will!

Champion Reading teaches you to become an active reader as opposed to the passive learner and reader you may be now. You will become information-targeted.

Champion Reading is also a course for busy people who have tasks to complete, process large amounts of information, and need to remember what they have read.

Champion Reading aids remedial readers to more easily decode words, sight read, increase vocabulary, look for main ideas, details, conclusions, inferences, and make judgments.

Champion Reading is not key word reading, skimming or skipping. We use a natural method – your hand. We work on natural focus, and you will see your material both vertically and horizontally. You will read for ideas, concepts, and main ideas. We use the precepts of Bloom's Taxonomy.

<u>Definition of an E-Learning Curve – Bloom's Taxonomy</u>

AN EXPLORATION OF THE RELATIONSHIP BETWEEN CHAMPION READING AND BLOOM'S TAXONOMY

KNOWLEDGE	• Mechanical Skills
COMPREHENSION	• "I understand what I read" • Discriminate for purpose • Mind Maps
APPLICATION	• Seeing parts of whole • Personal reading material • Mind Maps – the Champion Reading Method
SYNTHESIS	• Broad ideas from specifics • Return to Gestalt • "Great new ideas" • Verbalize impressions
EVALUATION	• Self-evaluation and internalization • Form judgments about impressions • Most enduring impressions

Bloom identified three domains of educational activities:

- Cognitive: mental skills (Knowledge)
- Affective: growth in feelings or emotional areas (Attitude)
- Psychomotor: manual or physical skills (Skills)

CHAPTER 9: How Do I Change from a Slow to a Fast Reader?

Well, it takes some dedicated practice time, belief, a desire to change, and patience. Yes, that is a tall order but if you first read through this book, and then follow the instructions during the three lessons, you will be a much improved reader.

Changing from slow reading to fast reading is not easy, and it engenders a total paradigm shift. You have to let go of your inner voice and get used to following your hand, as well as keeping up with the challenge of maintaining and increasing your speed.

Finding Your "Center"

Do you remember the day you suddenly were able to read, ride that bicycle without bumping into trees, swim without drowning, or hit that tennis ball? You don't know why, but one day you just "get it". That is "finding your center", or true synergy. The answer is sustained and constant practice, or for a lucky few, a natural ability. For most mortals it is sustained and constant practice.

When you do become a fast reader you will enter a zone we call tunnel vision, or total synergy. All you will see is the material, you will have total concentration, will hear no distracting noises, and your mind map will be amazing.

With Champion Reading you don't find your "center" until you reach a speed of about 800 words per minute. How do you get there? Well, it's called *sustained motion.* Sustained motion means you push yourself to attain 800 words per minute, *and stay at that speed for a while,* during the drills as outlined in the lessons provided at the end of this book.

Once this speed is attained you will see all the words, you will get the meaning of how the author wanted to tell you the story, and you will remember what you have read. This is because your mind will have filed the information in an orderly logical manner; therefore your retrieval of data is more efficient. After you have made a mind map, your recall will be much improved and eventually become excellent.

CHAPTER 10: The Need for Speed

Getting the skill to "come together"

When you are performing the drills don't worry about comprehension at first, just let your eyes, brain and hands work together.

In our live classes we like to use the analogy of the first time a new driver has to drive alone. The initial panic of "Oh, my goodness, will I remember to look in all the mirrors, turn on the direction signals, pay attention to who is in front, back and to the sides of my vehicle!!! AND figure out where I am going?" Now, when you have to drive it all seems to come together. Why? Because driving is a physical skill Reading is a physical skill. To get proficient at any physical skill you have to practice.

Repetition is the mother of skill.

Highly successful athletes work out and practice with their trainers and pros every single day. Performing the speed drills should be considered as *conditioning for your brain, and the mind maps as patterning for your thought processes. Creating mind maps helps you to create order out of chaos.*

You will need to have patience with yourself. Anything worth learning takes some effort.

The difference between TRY and TRIUMPH is a little "umph".

Remember, you think faster than you speak. At the beginning of this course you will be reading slowly, sounding out every word, and hearing your voice in your head. As you perform the drills repetitively, you will be able to let go of the voice in your head, and go faster. Don't slow yourself down. Once your eyes have seen the words they have entered your brain and you don't have to say them out loud or hear them. They have already entered your brain. As a beginning reader you were taught to say words out loud. That habit has kept you a slow reader with poor recall – that's almost over now!

Some habits that also hold us down are poor concentration, inadequate comprehension, regression, fixation, and inner speech. This course will help to eliminate these traits.

CHAPTER 11: Terminology Definitions

Comprehension is understanding what you are reading while you are reading it.

At first you will feel as if you do not comprehend anything you are reading, because you have been conditioned to read slowly in order to "get it". You will not feel you are really "reading". You are you just have not realized yet that your brain acknowledged recognition of the material.

We like to use the analogy of driving fast on a freeway, maybe going about 70 mph and then exiting to side roads, and having to slow down because it is a school zone. The speed is now 20 mph. Your frustration level can be intense. The point is that you see no more details of your surroundings at 20 mph than you did at 70 mph. As a matter of fact you were probably (hopefully) much more alert at 70 mph! You will experience a heightened sense of awareness because you are now concentrating more intensely.

Racetrack drivers see everything in their field of vision, and are able to make split second decisions at a high rate of speed. They become adept at this refined skill because they practice frequently, and their eyes and brains have become used to the elevated speed.

In the beginning you may experience some discomfort over your level of comprehension. It takes some practice and a level of sustained speed to finally convince your brain that it does not have to hear your inner voice.

Be reassured that you can "get it" if you persevere and release your need to hold on to your comforting auditory reassurance. Don't confuse the lack of hearing yourself say the words with not understanding what you are seeing.

You will not have impeccable comprehension at first. It may take until our third lesson before your mind maps are good. Judge yourself by the quantity of information you produce on your mind maps. You may feel that you have guessed at information and not be at all sure about the data you are recording. Sometimes you will perform one of the drills and inexplicably just blank out when it is time to write. This can be normal at first, and usually means you slowed down your speed without realizing it.

Because you have been conditioned to reading slowly since you first learned to read, your mind may take a little while to get over the panic, or comfort, of not hearing your voice in your head. The drills you will do in the lessons act as instruments of change.

A strange phenomenon occurs once you allow yourself to go fast. Hours or days after reading material that you were not sure you really "got", you may vividly remember details, concepts and main ideas.

Concentration is focusing on what you are reading and not getting distracted.

Regression is going back on a word or a line, and re-reading. The average person does this maybe 10-13 times per 100 words and finds out that 90% of the time they saw the material correctly the first time!

Regression tends to slow us down and muddle comprehension.

Sub-vocalization means that you are sounding out the words in your head while you are reading. You are limited to how fast you talk.

Subvocalization is defined as internal speech when reading a word. If you are reading at a speed of maybe 200 words per minute you are probably boring yourself to death while you are reading. This is why people fall asleep while reading, or come to the end of a page and have no idea what they looked at, etc.

Inner speech (subvocalizing) is where you feel you have to "hear" the words in your head otherwise you don't feel you have "got" it. This is usually a habit brought about because of the way most of us were taught to read. **Subvocalization** is present because of the sequential seeing, saying, hearing, knowing process of learning to read. It keeps you reading at rates comparable to hearing and speaking rather than to seeing and thinking rates. Although this habit can never be totally eradicated, it can be reduced.

Most people have **audio-visual dependency (sub-vocalization)** which is reading while "hearing" your voice in your head. This keeps you reading slowly and you tend to rely on one word at a time for meaning. In fact, you are reading no better than your grandparents did when they first learned to read.

Long-term retention is remembering what you have read or heard at a later time.

Mind wandering is daydreaming, or seeing a word while reading that causes you to digress and then you have to bring yourself back into the material

Fixation is when you stare at a word or phrase and go off into a daydream, and then have to re-read the text all over again.

Recall is being able to either write down or verbally do a tell-back in your own words as to what you have read, seen or heard. The average person forgets 50% of what they have read or heard after 1 hour.

The technology of reading has moved forward. You no longer communicate, work, study, do research, or learn in the same way you did ten years ago. Reading habits need to adapt and improve too.

Drawing inferences, arriving at conclusions, and coming to decisions is a skill. This becomes a value-added benefit for persevering with learning to become a Champion Reader. You are on your way to becoming an active as opposed to a passive reader and learner.

The average American reads anywhere from 80 to 350 words per minute, but the human brain can deal with, absorb and make decisions on between 8 – 10 thousand bits of data per second – hence you are boring yourself while you are reading so slowly.

CHAPTER 12: Why do I need to Speedread?

*Whatever you want to learn for the rest of your life –
there's a book, blog, website, etc., about it!*

It will be beneficial if you read faster so that you read with
greater clarity. We help you to achieve a form of tunnel
vision (so that it is you and the material only, and you are
not distracted by random thoughts, visual or aural
distractions). When a mind map is created from material
you have just read (or heard), you will remember the
material more accurately and for a longer period of time.
You will be cementing (inputting) the knowledge into your
long term memory.

It is a good idea to speed read if you have poor
concentration, sub-vocalization, regression, inadequate
recall and long-time retention plus mind wandering.
.

You can absorb and make decisions on 8 - 10,000 bits of
data per second. You need to speed read so that you can
transform from a passive to an active learner.

You need to speed read so that you take in entire thoughts
at a fast rate in order to get the essence of what the author is
conveying very quickly.

You need to speed read so that your concentration is more
focused.   Your comprehension improves when you
concentrate more intensely.

You need to speed read so that you keep up with all of your
reading and become successful at handling information.

Below is a chart and explanation detailing low concentration and mind wandering habits that occur with slow reading. These events happen at approximately 10 kb/second.

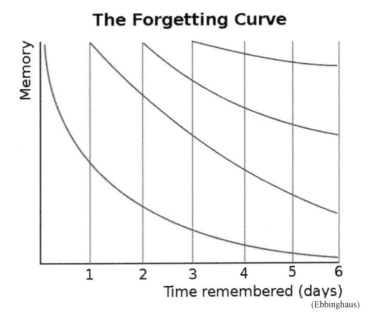

The Forgetting Curve

(Ebbinghaus)

The **forgetting curve** illustrates the decline of memory retention in time. A related concept is the **strength of memory** that refers to the durability that memory traces in the brain. The stronger the memory, the longer period of time that a person is able to recall it. A typical graph of the forgetting curve shows that humans tend to halve their memory of newly learned knowledge in a matter of days or weeks unless they consciously review the learned material.

In 1885, Hermann Ebbinghaus discovered the exponential nature of forgetting. The following formula can roughly describe it: $R = e^{-\frac{t}{s}}$ where R is memory retention, S is the relative strength of memory, and t is time.

The first significant study in this area was carried out by Hermann Ebbinghaus and published in 1885 as *Über das Gedächtnis* (later translated into English as *Memory: A Contribution to Experimental Psychology*). Ebbinghaus studied the memorization of nonsense syllables, such as "WID" and "ZOF". By repeatedly testing himself after various time periods and recording the results, he was the first to describe the shape of the forgetting curve.

Description

The speed of forgetting depends on a number of factors such as the difficulty of the learned material (e.g. how meaningful it is), its representation and physiological factors such as stress and sleep. The basal forgetting rate differs little between individuals. The difference in performance (e.g. at school) can be explained by mnemonic representation skills.

Basic training in mnemonic techniques can help overcome those differences in part. The best methods for increasing the strength of memory are:

1. better memory representation (e.g. with mnemonic techniques)
2. repetition based on active recall (esp. spaced repetition)

Each repetition in learning increases the optimum interval before the next repetition is needed (for near-perfect retention, initially repetitions may need to be made within days, but later they can be made after years).

There is debate among researchers about the shape of the curve for events and facts that are more significant to the subject. Some researchers, for example, suggest that memories for shocking events such as the Kennedy Assassination or 9/11 are vividly imprinted in memory. Others have compared contemporaneous written recollections with recollections recorded years later, and found considerable variations as the subject's memory incorporates after-acquired information. There is considerable research in this area as it relates to eyewitness identification testimony.

In a typical schoolbook application (e.g. learning word pairs), most students remember only 10% after 3–6 days (depending on the material). Therefore, 90% of what was learned is forgotten.

CHAPTER 13: Frequently Asked Questions:

Q. Do you see all the words?

A. Yes. With Champion Reading there is no skimming, scanning or key word reading. When you master this new skill you will read all the words.

Q. At what age is it appropriate for me to give this course to my children?

A. Children can be introduced to the skills by the time they are 6 years old. The readings contained in this course are suitable for students and adults who are reading at a 6th grade level and up.

Q. How can you appreciate fine literature so fast? (I love words.)

A. You get the author's style so much easier because it flows. The words have more beauty because you read them in context with one another instead of trying to memorize them one at a time, and from left to right. In fact, it will enhance the pleasure. The way you are currently reading, one word at a time, is slow and boring, plus it takes too long to get the meaning or the picture. Things can seem out of context. Champion Readers see whole groups of words, concepts, and the picture being put together.

Q. My teacher said it is impossible to read faster than 800 wpm. What's your position?

A. There are people who have been reading over 1000 wpm for years. President Kennedy was one of these "naturally fast readers". We have studied naturally fast readers and through many years of development, have incorporated their techniques into this course.

Q.   I had a friend who took a reading course and he's still reading the old way. Why?

A.   My suggestion to your friend would be to read this book, take this course, discover the changes, and spend more time developing the skill.

Q.   Can this help with math or chemistry textbooks, technical reading and study?

A.   Yes. You already read formulas and equations the Champion Reading way. Even though math and chemistry are technical materials, a large percentage of these materials are in paragraph- oriented form, which is quite adaptable to Champion Reading. Many of our graduates are students and professional people.

This book covers the basic skills of Champion Reading. Our Advanced Champion Reading book teaches technical reading, and contains our textbook attack method.

Q.   Do I always use my hand?

A.   Yes. You always use your hand as a pacer that is what forces your eyes to be attracted to the print on the page and stay focused. This helps your concentration which gives you better comprehension.

Q.   Do you see the whole page at once?

A.   It is possible with practice for you to see an entire page. It requires mastery of the skill.

Q.   Do you see the width of the line?

A.   Seeing the entire width of a line is no problem.

Q.   *Does it work in another language?*
A.   Yes, as long as you are proficient in that language.

Q.   *How fast will I be able to read?*
A.   You will have a reading range. Much depends upon the vocabulary used in the material being read. Obviously, the more familiar you are with the vocabulary the faster you will read often by the words around it, you can discern the meaning. Of course, if you still don't understand the meaning, by all means stop and consult the dictionary.

You cannot remember what you did not understand.

Q.   *What does I.Q. have to do with learning the skill?*
A.   Nothing. Anything you can read slowly you can be taught to read quickly. I.Q. has nothing to do with developing the skill. This is simply a physical skill, which requires practice. It has nothing to do with sex, race, age, I.Q., socio-economic groupings or even levels of education.

Q.   *What effect would my defective vision have on acquiring the skill? (One eye, dyslexia, tunnel vision, bi-focals)*
A.   It depends on the problem. Most dyslexia-challenged students learn and thrive with Champion Reading. Tunnel vision is one problem where we might not be able to help. With Champion Reading you develop the skill you already have; you learn to read groups of words at one time. You see the words vertically, horizontally and peripherally at the same time, just as you see things all day long. Wearing glasses is not a problem.

Q.   *Do you retain the skill?*

A.   As long as you use the skill it will be there for you. It's when you take your hand off the page for a long period of time that you might notice a regression. This skill is like learning to ride a bike or to tie your shoes. It's always there. You never completely lose the skill. It would never take you 10 hours of class time, plus the practice to redevelop the skill. This is just like any other skill, you have to use it. If you stop reading, naturally the skill will lessen. If you don't read for work or school, at least read newspapers or magazines. Any reading will keep the skill fresh

Q.   *Will I be able to do my homework during the home practice?*

A.   Not at first. The first few lessons will be teaching you new techniques, and you will be doing a practice drill where you will be trained to see words and go at a rate faster than you can presently read. We will be teaching you a preliminary technique to use when you read, and this will be in addition to the home practice.

Q.   *Does my present reading speed determine what my new speed will be?*

A.   Generally, no. Your attitude and application are more important factors. Learning to be a Champion Reader is more dependent upon attitude and application than upon I.Q. or initial reading speed.

Q.   *Will this new skill change my old habits?*

A.   Definitely, if you want to change your old reading habits.

Q.   *How do I measure comprehension?*

A.   Comprehension understands what you are reading while you are reading it; recall is remembering what you have read. Mental, verbal and written tell-backs are measuring methods. No single test or single reading measures thoroughly either comprehension or recall.

Q.   *What happens when I come across an unfamiliar word?*

A.   Continue reading and see if the context tells you the definition. If not, stop and look the word up in a dictionary. Remember that the chief function of a dictionary is to give contexts for a word and that reading also does this. Resorting to a dictionary too frequently destroys the "flow of reading".

Q.   *When I read fast will I retain well?*

A.   Generally, yes, more than a slow reader. The rate of retention for a fast reader is rather high. Champion Reading, with a Mind Map, has been proven to often help people learn well. Champion Readers usually test better.

CHAPTER 14: Let's get started!

You will need:

- Please go to our website: **www.championreading.com** and download a copy of the Blank Mind Map and the Daily Drill practice record sheet.

- A timer that can be set to beep or buzz at the end of one minute.
- A calculator
- An easy reading novel (don't try to learn this skill at first with any other type of material)
- 3 paper clips or sticky flags
- Paper
- Pencils

FINDING YOUR BEGINNING SPEED

To calculate your speed (words per minute WPM) in your own novel you need to first **count every word in three full lines of the following article, and divide by three** to get your words per line (WPL). We would normally do this for you, but because of the varying formats to be used to deliver this material to you, it is more foolproof that you calculate this yourself. Please make a note of this number.

In order to find your beginning speed you will set your timer for **one minute** and proceed to read the following article. Please read the way you **normally** read for what you consider **very good** comprehension. At the end of the minute please make a mark where you finished reading.

COMPUTERS

Champion Reading At Work
By Jennifer Wozny,
Founder Power Learning

The on-line text moves so fast you are able to read, understand and explain it in detail. People's voices come through your computer. You see their faces on screen as they speak. The future has arrived. Are you feeling a little overwhelmed?

You are in a technology and information explosion. Consider your competitors and co-workers reading at just such a pace with the current print and non-print media. Can you keep pace and excel in such a work setting? Of course you can, with some training. Check out Champion Reading.

You read and scan numerous trade periodicals to stay abreast of the cutting edge in your field. Undoubtedly you use a computer, PDA or telephone to store vital bits of information for later use. Memos you need to read and respond to cover your desk. Emails are proliferating hourly on your computer.

Your position is full of challenge and complexities that make you reach deeper within yourself for more.

You live in a fast paced, technology sensitive world. The workplace is changing. In order to stay competitive you must be an informed team player who has sharpened her/his skills to their finest.

Continuing education is an integral part of the work environment. You strive for excellence, quality, and collaboration. Your goal: to excel individually and with your team in the workplace.

So much to read and so little time! Do you find yourself taking things home to read after work, only to bring them back to the office still unread? Are you staying late to read or reread vital documents? There is a solution.

Enter Champion Reading.

To keep our corporations and other businesses flourishing, we must stay at the cutting edge of technology and talent. Business must train and/or hire those who can do it better. Many companies have brought Champion Reading in to do just that.

People are business's most valuable resource. Having a well trained staff is vital. Imagine a staff that could read and comprehend at least 30% better than presently. How much more could be accomplished? What impact would that have on the bottom line? How would it impact the competitive edge of that company?

So much to read and so little time! Being a professional involves considerable amounts of reading. You must be knowledgeable of current and future trends. So you read trade journals, periodicals, books, reports, memos, etc., of varying lengths regularly, almost religiously. You must stay on top of new information to retain your competitive edge.

Have you ever wondered how some people read so fast yet understand and retain what they read? By taking a speed reading course, some individuals distance themselves far ahead of the pack. This is the skill to have for this 21st century. Learning it now can help you stay competent.

As a manger, business owner, department or project manager, or other person with tremendous amounts of reading on the job, can you afford to continue reading and rereading material to gain the information that you seek?

From the first day you learned to read the technology of reading has changed. Yes, you got a little faster and increased your vocabulary but now new skills are available to learn to vastly increase the volume that you can consume. Just accessing a search engine now is mind boggling – the possibilities are endless for information acquisition.

There are techniques to assist you in wading through the barrage of information, sift through the extraneous, and retain those important facts that may help you clinch a new deal, make that first impression, sharpen your wit, and increase your business savvy!

Speed reading can do many things for many people. The business professional who is taking college courses for an advanced degree will get through challenging textbooks in less time, make appropriate notes, and retain key points for testing or business use.

Not only can speed reading save precious time, increase retention of important information, but show you how to take better notes. It can also help you to determine when to skim, and read for maximum comprehension in addition to other benefits.

Speed reading can open up blocks of time that you can devote to a new job skill or goal to expand your current business activities and positively impact the bottom line. As employees are more productive, the firm is more productive.

As companies continue to downsize, you may need to sharpen your job skills. Make yourself more attractive to your employer now. Increase your output by being able to read and handle more information. Many people now handle the work that 2 or 3 employees used to do ten years ago.

Should you get that pink slip, you are a prime candidate for speed reading. Not only will it help your reading speed and increase comprehension, your reading confidence can soar as well. It increases your attractiveness to future employers.

A straight-A college student took a speed reading course so that he could have more free time to spend with his fiancée. In addition to saving him time in note taking and reading, he has more free time. A luxury we can all enjoy.

We are in an information explosion. It will only accelerate as we move further through this century.

Are you ready?

Benefits of Champion Reading:
- **Increased reading speed**
- **Increased comprehension**
- **Increased retention**
- **Increased productivity**
- **Reduction of time necessary to read a document**
- **More time for other tasks**
- **Elimination of dread of reading**
- **Increased confidence**
- **Better job skills**

Champion Reading is suitable for anyone aged 11 on up who wants to increase their reading rate and get more out of what they read. It has helped students and business professionals in Houston, Texas for over thirty years. It can help you.

STOP

Please compute your speed (words per minute) by counting the lines you just read in this last minute and then multiply that number by how many words per line there are in the above article.

Please make multiple copies of the following Daily Drill Practice Record Sheet for your future use.

Please make a note of this number on your Daily Drill Practice Record Sheet as this signifies your beginning speed. Formula is # of lines read, multiplied by average words per line. If you read 25 lines just now, and your average words per line was 10, then your beginning speed would be 250 words per minute. (25x10=250).

Please go to our website **www.championreading.com** in order to; download a printable copy of the following document

CHAMPION READING
DAILY DRILL PRACTICE RECORD SHEET

BEGINNING SPEED_____   DATE STARTED COURSE _____

DATE	DRILL	SPEED	MIND MAP DATA (names/events/setting)

CHAPTER 15: Lesson 1

Lesson Plan

1. Finding your beginning speed
2. Introduction to Daily Drill Practice Record Sheet
3. How to Hold a Book and Turn Pages
4. Hand motions
5. How to calculate speed.
6. Information on why we use hand motions, and drills
7. Introduction to basic Champion Reading Drill

1. FINDING YOUR BEGINNING SPEED

Please enter your beginning speed on your daily sheet as outlined above.

2. DAILY DRILL PRACTICE RECORD SHEET

The Daily Practice Record Sheet is self-explanatory and should be used to record all of the drills you perform. Please make multiple copies for your future use.

3. HOW TO HOLD A BOOK AND TURN PAGES

If your book is a paperback and new, it will help if you make it more pliable by flicking the pages back and forth and by opening the book at random and attempting to flatten the spine of the book.

To hold the book correctly, place your left hand across the top of the book and turn the pages with your left hand using your middle finger and thumb as shown visually. The only function of your left hand is to turn pages, and the only function of your right hand is to use the hand motion.

Holding the open book flat down on your table, hold top of book down with forearm thumb and forefinger positioned near upper right-hand corner, to turn pages, OR hold book down by placing left arm along top margin with thumb near middle of right-hand page and middle finger extended to lift page at corner.

This method is for both right and left handed people. OPTIONAL for left-handers: turn pages from top or bottom with right hand while pacing with left hand.

This works equally well if you are reading a hardback book, textbook, large paperback, or very thin book.

4. BROAD UNDERLINING HANDMOTION

With your right hand make a circle with your thumb and forefinger, and leave your remaining three fingers straight and together as shown. (This is the "AOK" sign).

Place your hand on your book with the three straight fingers underneath the first word on the first line in your book. Go from the beginning to the end of the line, from left to right, underneath the line, on every line in a smooth, sweeping motion, touching the page as if you were dusting the page. Your eyes should be focused above your middle finger. We call this the Broad Underlining Hand motion

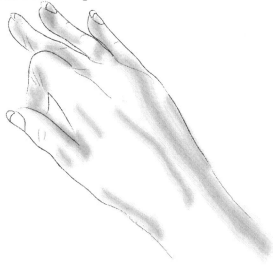

50

```
┌─────────────────────────────────────┐
│ BROAD UNDERLINING                     │
│                                       │
│ XXXXXXXXXXXXXXXXXXXXXXXXXX            │
│ XXXXXXXXXXXXXXXXXXXXXXXXXX            │
│ XXXXXXXXXXXXXXXXXXXXXXXXXX            │
│ XXXXXXXXXXXXXXXXXXXXXXXXXX            │
│ XXXXXXXXXXXXXXXXXXXXXXXXXX            │
│                                       │
│ Make "AOK" sign. Palm down.           │
│ From beginning to end of line.        │
│ Raise at end of line. Use for text.   │
└─────────────────────────────────────┘
```

5. HOW TO CALCULATE SPEED

To calculate your speed (words per minute WPM) in your own novel; you need to first count every word in three full lines of a typical page, or document, and divide by three to get your words per line (WPL).

It would also be helpful to count every line on a typical page. It is only necessary to do this **once per book.** Make a note of these numbers.

If you are doing a drill and wish to find out your speed then you count how many lines you read and multiply that number by how many words per line.

For example: John read three pages in the last of the Champion Reading Drill. There are 35 lines on a page, with 10 words per line. His speed is 1050 words per minute. (35x10x3 =1050).

6. WHY WE USE HANDMOTIONS AND DRILLS

The purpose is to get you faster and faster so that you become familiar with holding the book, turning the pages, and seeing words very quickly. Eventually you will stop, or greatly lessen, your audio-visual dependency which is hearing the words in your head. This is also the drill you should use for extra practice.

One of the basic tenets of the course is the fact that we have to teach you to speed up your reading. Without high speed your concentration is not sharp or acute. One very important way to do that is to give you speed drills and teach you mind mapping. Until you reach about 800 words per minute for good comprehension, you will not really be seeing and remembering a lot of material. Persevere with the following drills and mind maps and you will be successful.

The methods to teach you this course are drills, visual concepts, making use of vertical vision, helping you create a more efficient storage system for information to give you quicker and more accurate retrieval. Follow the steps, do the drills in the sequence presented, and become a Champion reader!

For extra practice, any time, and as often as you can, do the Champion Reading Drill in its entirety.

It is recommended you do these lessons one week apart but practice the Champion Reading Drill daily as many times as you can

7. INTRODUCTION TO CHAMPION READING DRILL (CRD)

Before we start, select your book, have three paperclips or sticky flags ready, and print a Blank Mind Map or draw one on paper. Count every word in three full lines of your book and divide by three. This is your average words per line (WPL). Make a note of this number. Now count every line on a full page of your book. This is your lines per page (LPP). Make a note of this number.

We are now ready to begin:

Insert a paperclip where you are going to begin at the start at a new chapter in your novel. You are going to be reading for a total of 6 minutes where you will not stop, take a break, or have any interruptions. The purpose is to introduce you to some techniques for intense concentration.

RULES:

- Don't stop.
- Don't go back or reread a word or a line.
- Always use your hand.
- Don't allow any distractions as you have to go from Step A through to Step F without a break. You are looking for momentum.

CHAMPION READING DRILL (CRD)
Hand motion is Broad Underlining

This is the order of the drill:

A. Read 1 minute for GOOD comprehension
B. Re-read 1 minute for FAIR comprehension (3 lines further)
C. Re-read 1 minute for FAIR comprehension (5 lines further)
D. Double your reading - LOW comprehension
E. Add 1 more page to your reading - LOW comprehension
F. Read 1 minute NEW material, GOOD comprehension

Count lines you read in F, multiply by words per line, record this total on your Daily Drill Practice Record Sheet

DIRECTIONS

We are assuming that you have inserted your first paperclip (or sticky flag) on page 1 of your practice novel. We are now going to read for one minute, **using the Broad Underlining Hand motion (hand in AOK mode)** one line at a time, from the beginning to the end of the line, underneath the line as if you are dusting. We are going for GOOD comprehension which for our purpose at this time means simply "I understand the words I am reading as I am reading them".

A. Insert beginning clip, set your timer for one minute and read 1 minute for GOOD comprehension. When your timer beeps insert 2nd clip where you just ended.

B. Go back to the beginning clip, set your timer for one minute and read 1 minute for FAIR comprehension, trying to go 3 lines further than your second clip. When your timer beeps at the end of the minute, move your 2nd clip to where you just ended.

C. Go back to the beginning clip, set your timer for one minute and re-read for 1 minute for FAIR comprehension, trying to go 5 lines further. When your timer beeps at the end of the minute, move your 2nd clip to where you ended.

D. Go back to the beginning clip, double the number of lines or pages you just read, leave 1st clip and 2nd clip in, and insert 3rd clip **at your new goal**. (Whatever amount you have just read, please double that amount). Set your timer for one minute and read very fast with LOW comprehension. The goal is to just get to the third clip by the time your timer beeps. Maybe you will see very little, but just strive to get to the ending third clip! When your timer beeps at the end of the minute leave your 3rd clip where it was placed, even if you did not achieve success at this time.

E. Add one more page to the number of pages you just read, leave 1st and 2nd clips in, and **move your 3rd clip** to reflect where your goal is. Set your timer for one minute, go back to your first clip and read very fast with LOW comprehension. Again, your only goal is to move fast and get to the ending clip in one minute. When your timer beeps at the end of the minute take out your 1st and 2nd paperclips, and move your 3rd paperclip to where you just finished.

F. Turn to where your 3rd paperclip is in your book. Now set your timer for one minute and read for 1 minute with GOOD comprehension, in new material.

Calculate your speed by counting how many lines you just read in this last minute only, (F), and multiplying that number by how many words per line there are in your novel. Enter this on your Daily Drill Practice Record Sheet.

Please repeat this drill one more time to Complete Lesson One.

HOW TO DO EXTRA PRACTICE

Use the Champion Reading Drill between lessons 1 and 2 for your daily practice as many times as you can.

CHAPTER 16: Lesson Two

Lesson Plan

1. Introduction to Mind Mapping
2. Champion Reading Drill with mind mapping
3. Record
4. Champion Acceleration drill
5. Record
6. Champion Reading Drill with mind mapping
7. Record
8. Extra Practice

1. INTRODUCTION TO MIND MAPPING

The Mind Map enables you to start seeing the reading process not just as a lot of words, but as MEANING. The Mind Maps are a tool to use to remember what you have read.

In creating Mind Maps, first look for major divisions. In a chapter of a novel, these would be the scenes of the chapter.

Your preview must establish what the most important information is.   Once you find this information, condense it into a few key words which add to your understanding. You must understand what you have read in order to condense it.

You should then read for supportive information, again condensing the new material into key words and adding them by connecting lines. It is very important that everything be connected by lines so that nothing is lost to the eye.

Remember that it is not the purpose of a Mind Map to record everything. Rather, it is to record key facts and information so that when you see it later you will remember more of what you learned.

A Mind Map is a special method for saving and remembering information.

Use key words or phrases, no complete sentences. Example would be if you read the following "the black and white dog sat on the red and green mat and proceeded to wash its paws......" you would put the word "dog" under Characters, the word "mat" under Setting, and the word "wash" under Events. If it was important to identify which dog or which mat, then do so.

Very simply, under Characters enter any living person or animal, or an identifier if no name is given to you, e.g., boy in park, lady with red hat, etc. Under Setting enter where your characters were, as well as any mood or emotions that occurred, and under Events enter anything that your characters either did or events that happened to them. (Past, present or what may happen in the future).

Below is a Blank Mind Map, and also a Mind Map filled in with where information goes on your mind map.

This is for remembering what you have read in an organized fashion so that your retrieval is more orderly and efficient. Mind Maps work on trains of thought, triggers for the brain, and memory hooks.

Remember, on a Mind Map you are not writing sentences - you are writing a few key words to remind yourself what you saw

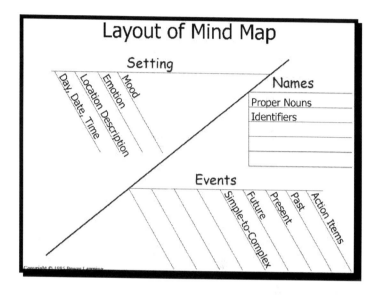

Please go to our website **www.championreading.com** in order to download a printable copy of the following document. It is necessary for you to make multiple copies of the blank Mind Map for your use.

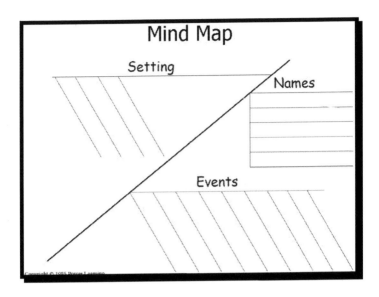

Mind Map

Setting

Names

Events

Copyright © 1985 Power Learning

2. CHAMPION READING DRILL
    Hand motion is Broad Underlining

    This is the order of the drill:

    A. Read 1 minute for GOOD comprehension

    B. Re-read 1 minute for FAIR comprehension (5 lines further)

    C. Re-read 1 minute for FAIR comprehension (10 lines further)

    D. Double your reading - LOW comprehension

    E. Add 2 more pages to your reading – LOW comprehension

F. Read 1 minute NEW material, GOOD comprehension.

Enter on a fresh Mind Map everything you think you saw during your journey from step A through step F.

Count lines you read in F, multiply by words per line, record this total on Daily Drill Practice Record Sheet. Please also record how many names, events and setting items you managed to write on your Mind Map.

DIRECTIONS

A. Insert beginning clip, set your timer for one minute and read 1 minute for GOOD comprehension. When your timer beeps insert 2nd clip where you just ended. When your timer beeps insert 2nd clip where you just ended.

B. Go back to the beginning clip, set your timer for one minute and read 1 minute for FAIR comprehension, trying to go 5 lines further than your second clip. When your timer beeps at the end of the minute, move your 2nd clip to where you just ended.

C. Go back to the beginning clip, set your timer for one minute and re-read for 1 minute for FAIR comprehension, trying to go 10 lines further. When your timer beeps at the end of the minute, move your 2nd clip to where you ended.

D. Go back to the beginning clip, double the number of lines or pages you just read, leave 1st clip and 2nd clip in, and insert 3rd clip to your new goal.

(Whatever amount you have just read, please double that amount). Set your timer for one minute and read very fast with LOW comprehension. The goal is to just get to the third clip by the time your timer beeps. Maybe you will see very little, but just strive to get to the ending third clip! When your timer beeps at the end of the minute leave your 3rd clip where it was placed, even if you did not achieve success at this time.

E. Add two more pages to the number of pages you just read, leave 1st and 2nd clips in, and move your 3rd clip to reflect where your goal is. Set your timer for one minute, go back to your first clip and read very fast with LOW comprehension. Again, your only goal is to move fast and get to the ending clip in one minute. When your timer beeps at the end of the minute take out your 1st and 2nd paperclips, and move your 3rd paperclip to where you just finished.

F. Turn to where your 3rd paperclip is in your book. Now set your timer for one minute and read for 1 minute with GOOD comprehension, in new material.

Enter on a fresh Mind Map everything you think you saw during your journey from step A through step F.

Calculate your speed by counting how many lines you just read in this last minute only, (F), and multiplying that number by how many words per line there are in your novel.

3. RECORD

   Enter this number on your Daily Drill Practice Record Sheet. Please also record how many names, events and setting items you managed to write on your Mind Map.

4. CHAMPION READING ACCELERATION DRILL
   Broad Underlining Hand motion

   This is the order of the drill.

   A. Read 30 seconds
   B. Mind Map 30 seconds
   C. Continue reading 1 minute
   D. Add to Mind Map 1 minute
   E. Continue reading 1.5 minutes
   F. Add to Mind Map 1.5 minutes
   G. Insert paperclip where ended, read 2 minutes
   H. Add to Mind Map 2 minutes.
   I. Calculate speed in last 2 minutes, record. Count number of names, events and settings, record.

   For this drill you will need an easy-reading novel, 2 paperclips, and a mind map blank.

   Open your book and find where you wish to start. This drill will help you see data and remember it. Don't split this drill up and don't read slowly. You will be able to write more the faster you go. No clips in the book at this time. Please note that in this drill you are reading continuously through the book, no re-reading, and go as fast as you can.

DIRECTIONS

A. Set your timer for 30 seconds. Read as fast as you can, using the Broad Underlining Hand motion. Stop when you hear your buzzer.

B. Set your timer for another 30 seconds, and start writing on your mind map.

C. When you hear the buzzer stop writing, and set your timer for one minute. Pick your book up, find where you left off and now read for a minute even faster.

D. Stop when your buzzer sounds, set your buzzer for one minute, turn the book over, and add to your mind map. Try adding one more name, one more event, and one more item on setting.

E. Stop when your buzzer goes off and now set your timer for one and a half minutes. Pick your book up and find where you left off, try going faster than you want to go - just see what you get!

F. Stop when your timer goes off and set your timer for one and a half minutes, turn the book over and add to your mind map! Go for one more name you might have seen, one more event, and one more piece of information for setting, remember you are putting down description of location, dates, times, mood, emotions!

Stop when your timer buzzes.

G. Pick up your book, insert a paperclip where you left off, and set your timer for two minutes. You are now going to go even faster for 2 minutes. You are just looking for who, what, where, and when!

H. Stop when your timer goes off. Put a second paperclip where you just finished. Set your timer for two minutes. Turn your book over, add to your mind map - put down as much as you can. Read what you have written for events - did something else happen because of what you wrote down - if it did, add it to the mind map. How about more in setting - what was it like where your characters were, was it hot, cold, clean, dirty - were they happy, sad, angry, frightened - do you know the name of where they were, the city, country, period of world history, etc. put it down under setting. How about one more name.

I. Stop when your timer goes off.

5. RECORD

Multiply how many pages you just read in these last 2 minutes by how many lines per page and how many words per line and enter this number on your Daily Drill Practice Record Sheet. You may want to also keep a record of how many names you put down as well as events and settings and compare this after you do this drill several times.

6. CHAMPION READING DRILL

Hand motion is Broad Underlining

This is the order of the drill:

A. Read 1 minute for GOOD comprehension
B. Re-read 1 minute for FAIR comprehension (5 lines further)
C. Re-read 1 minute for FAIR comprehension (10 lines further)
D. Double your reading - LOW comprehension
E. Add 2 more pages to your reading - LOW comprehension
F. Read 1 minute NEW material, GOOD comprehension.

Enter on a fresh Mind Map everything you think you saw during your journey from step A through step F.

Count lines you read in F, multiply by words per line, record this total on Daily Drill Practice Record Sheet. Please also record how many names, events and setting items you managed to write on your Mind Map.

DIRECTIONS

A. Insert beginning clip, set your timer for one minute and read 1 minute for GOOD comprehension. When your timer beeps insert 2nd clip where you just ended. When your timer beeps insert 2nd clip where you just ended.

B. Go back to the beginning clip, set your timer for one minute and read 1 minute for FAIR comprehension, trying to go 5 lines further than your second clip. When your timer beeps at the end of the minute, move your 2nd clip to where you just ended.

C. Go back to the beginning clip, set your timer for one minute and re-read for 1 minute for FAIR comprehension, trying to go 10 lines further. When your timer beeps at the end of the minute, move your 2nd clip to where you ended.

D. Go back to the beginning clip, double the number of lines or pages you just read, leave 1st clip and 2nd clip in, and insert 3rd clip to your new goal. (Whatever amount you have just read, please double that amount). Set your timer for one minute and read very fast with LOW comprehension. The goal is to just get to the third clip by the time your timer beeps. Maybe you will see very little, but just strive to get to the ending third clip! When your timer beeps at the end of the minute leave your 3rd clip where it was placed, even if you did not achieve success at this time.

E. Add two more pages to the number of pages you just read, leave 1st and 2nd clips in, and move your 3rd clip to reflect where your goal is. Set your timer for one minute, go back to your first clip and read very fast with LOW comprehension. Again, your only goal is to move fast and get to the ending clip in one minute. When your timer beeps at the end of the minute take out your 1st and 2nd paperclips, and move your 3rd paperclip to where you just finished.

F. Turn to where your 3rd paperclip is in your book. Now set your timer for one minute and read for 1 minute with GOOD comprehension, in new material.

G. Enter on a fresh Mind Map everything you think you saw during your journey from step A through step F.

H. Calculate your speed by counting how many lines you just read in this last minute only, (F), and multiplying that number by how many words per line there are in your novel.

7. RECORD

Enter this number on your Daily Drill Practice Record Sheet. Please also record how many names, events and setting items you managed to write on your Mind Map.

8. EXTRA PRACTICE

Again, please practice the Champion Reading Drill daily.

CHAPTER 17: Lesson 3

Lesson Plan

1. Champion Reading Drill
2. Record
3. Champion Acceleration Drill
4. Record
5. Champion Reading Drill
6. Record

1. CHAMPION READING DRILL (CRD)
   This is the order of the drill:

   A. Read 1 minute for GOOD comprehension

   B. Re-read 1 minute for FAIR comprehension (10 lines further)

   C. Re-read 1 minute for FAIR comprehension (15 lines further)

   D. Double your reading - LOW comprehension

   E. Add 2 more pages to your reading - LOW comprehension

   F. Read 1 minute NEW material, GOOD comprehension.

   G. Count lines you read in F, multiply by words per line, record this total on Daily Drill Practice Record Sheet.

DIRECTIONS

A. Insert beginning clip, set your timer for one minute and read 1 minute for GOOD comprehension. When your timer beeps insert 2nd clip where you just ended.

B. Go back to the beginning clip, set your timer for one minute and read 1 minute for FAIR comprehension, trying to go 10 lines further than your second clip. When your timer beeps at the end of the minute, move your 2nd clip to where you just ended.

C. Go back to the beginning clip, set your timer for one minute and re-read for 1 minute for FAIR comprehension, trying to go 15 lines further. When your timer beeps at the end of the minute, move your 2nd clip to where you ended.

D. Go back to the beginning clip, double the number of lines or pages you just read, leave 1st clip and 2nd clip in, and insert 3rd clip to your new goal. (Whatever amount you have just read, please double that amount). Set your timer for one minute and read very fast with LOW comprehension. The goal is to just get to the third clip by the time your timer beeps. Maybe you will see very little, but just strive to get to the ending third clip! When your timer beeps at the end of the minute leave your 3rd clip where it was placed, even if you did not achieve success at this time.

E. Add two more pages to the number of pages you just read, leave 1st and 2nd clips in, and move your 3rd clip to reflect where your goal is. Set your timer for one minute, go back to your first clip and read very fast with LOW comprehension. Again, your only goal is to move fast and get to the ending clip in one minute. When your timer beeps at the end of the minute take out your 1st and 2nd paperclips, and move your 3rd paperclip to where you just finished.

G. Turn to where your 3rd paperclip is in your book. Now set your timer for one minute and read for 1 minute with GOOD comprehension, in new material.

Calculate your speed by counting how many lines you just read in this last minute only, (F), and multiplying that number by how many words per line there are in your novel.

2. RECORD

Enter this on your Daily Drill Practice Record Sheet.

3. CHAMPION READING ACCELERATION DRILL

This is the order of the drill

A. Read 30 seconds
B. Mind Map 30 seconds
C. Continue reading 1 minute
D. Add to Mind Map 1 minute
E. Continue reading 1.5 minutes

F. Add to Mind Map 1.5 minutes
G. Insert paperclip where ended, read 2 minutes
H. Add to Mind Map 2 minutes.
I. Calculate speed in last 2 minutes, record.
J. Count number of names, events and settings, record.

DIRECTIONS

For this drill you will need an easy-reading novel, 2 paperclips, and a mind map blank.

Open your book and find where you wish to start. This drill will help you see data and remember it. Don't split this drill up and don't read slowly. You will be able to write more the faster you go. No clips in the book at this time. Find where you wish to begin. Please note that in this drill you are reading continuously through the book, no re-reading, and go as fast as you can.

A. Set your timer for 30 seconds. Read as fast as you can. Stop when you hear your buzzer. Set it for another 30 seconds, and start writing on your mind map.

B. When you hear the buzzer stop writing, and set your timer for one minute. Pick your book up, find where you left off and now read for a minute even faster.

C. Stop when your buzzer sounds, set your buzzer for one minute, turn the book over, and add to your mind map.

D. Try adding one more name, one more event, and one more item on setting.

E. Stop when your buzzer goes off and now set your timer for one and a half minutes. Pick your book up and find where you left off, try going faster than you want to go - just see what you get!

F. Stop when your timer goes off and set your timer for one and a half minutes,

G. Turn the book over and add to your mind map! Go for one more name you might have seen, one more event, and one more piece of information for setting; remember you are putting down description of location, dates, times, mood, emotions!

H. Stop when your timer buzzes.

I. Pick up your book, insert a paperclip where you left off, and set your timer for two minutes. You are now going to go even faster for 2 minutes. You are just looking for who, what, where, and when!

J. Stop when your timer goes off. Set your timer for two minutes. Turn your book over, add to your mind map - put down as much as you can. Read what you have written for events - did something else happen because of what you wrote down - if it did, add it to the mind map. How about more in setting - what was it like where your characters were, was it hot, cold, clean, dirty - were they happy, sad, angry, frightened - do you know the name of where they were, the city, country, period

of world history, etc. put it down under setting..
How about one more name.

K. Stop when your timer goes off.   Put a second
paperclip in your book where you just finished.

4.   RECORD

Multiply how many pages you just read in these last 2
minutes by how many lines per page and how many
words per line and enter this number on your Daily
Drill Practice Record Sheet.   You may want to also
keep a record of how many names you put down as
well as events and settings and compare this after you
do this drill several times.

5.   CHAMPION READING DRILL (CRD)

This is the order of the drill:

A.   Read 1 minute for GOOD comprehension

B.   Re-read 1 minute for FAIR comprehension (15
lines further)

C.   Re-read 1 minute for FAIR comprehension (20
lines further)

D.   Double your reading - LOW comprehension

E.   Add 3 more pages to your reading - LOW
comprehension

F.   Read 1 minute NEW material, GOOD
comprehension

Count lines you read in F, multiply by words per line, record this total on Daily Drill Practice Record Sheet.

DIRECTIONS

A. Insert beginning clip, set your timer for one minute and read 1 minute for GOOD comprehension. When your timer beeps, insert 2nd clip where you just ended.

B. Go back to the beginning clip, set your timer for one minute and read 1 minute for FAIR comprehension, trying to go 15 lines further than your second clip. When your timer beeps at the end of the minute, move your 2nd clip to where you just ended.

C. Go back to the beginning clip, set your timer for one minute and re-read for 1 minute for FAIR comprehension, trying to go 20 lines further. When your timer beeps at the end of the minute, move your 2nd clip to where you ended.

D. Go back to the beginning clip, double the number of lines or pages you just read, leave 1st clip and 2nd clip in, and insert 3rd clip to your new goal. (Whatever amount you have just read, please double that amount). Set your timer for one minute and read very fast with LOW comprehension. The goal is to just get to the third clip by the time your timer beeps. Maybe you will see very little, but just strive to get to the ending third clip! When your timer beeps at the end of the minute leave your 3rd clip where it was placed, even if you did not achieve success at this time.

E. Add three more pages to the number of pages you just read, leave 1st and 2nd clips in, and move your 3rd clip to reflect where your goal is. Set your timer for one minute, go back to your first clip and read very fast with LOW comprehension. Again, your only goal is to move fast and get to the ending clip in one minute. When your timer beeps at the end of the minute take out your 1st and 2nd paperclips, and move your 3rd paperclip to where you just finished.

F. Turn to where your 3rd paperclip is in your book. Now set your timer for one minute and read for 1 minute with GOOD comprehension, in new material.

G. Calculate your speed by counting how many lines you just read in this last minute only, (F), and multiplying that number by how many words per line there are in your novel.

6. RECORD

Enter this on your Daily Drill Practice Record Sheet.

CHAPTER 18: Recommendations for
Maintaining Your Skill

We recommend doing the Champion Reading Drill daily, and that you try to push your speed in step (F) of the drill to around 800 - 1500 wpm. Do this Drill as often as you can.

Congratulations! Continue doing the practice, use your hand for all your reading and adapt your speed faster and faster as you become more confident.

Chapter 19: RECOMMENDED READING LIST

- ALCOTT, LOUISA MAY
    - *Little Women; Little Men*
- ASIMOV, ISAAC
    - *The Currents of Space*
    - plus others
- AUSTEN, JANE
    - *Pride and Prejudice*
- BENET, STEPHEN
    - *John Brown's Body*
- BLACKMORE, JOHN
    - *Lorna Doone*
- BOWEN, ELIZABETH
    - *A House in Paris*
- BRADBURY, RAY:
    - *Dandelion Wine*
    - plus others
- BRONTE, CHARLOTTE
    - *Jane Eyre*
- BRONTE, EMILY
    - *Wuthering Heights*
- BUCK, PEARL
    - *Dragon Seed*
    - *The Good Earth*
- BUNYAN, JOHN
    - *Pilgrim's Progress*
- BUTLER, SAMUEL
    - *The Way of All Flesh*
- CAMUS, ALBERT
    - *The Rebel*
    - *The Plague*
    - *The Stranger*

- CATHER, WILLA
  - *Death Comes to the Archbishop*
  - *My Antonio*
- CERVANTES, MIGUEL
  - *Don Quixote*
- CHESTERTON, G.K
  - *The Man Who Was Thursday*
  - *Ballad of the White House*
- CLARK, WALTER VAN TILLBERY
  - *The Ox-Bow Incident*
- CLARKE, ARTHUR C.
  - *My Childhood's End*
  - *2001, A Space Odyssey*
  - plus others
- CONRAD, JOSEPH
  - *Almayer's Folly*
  - *Lord Jim*
  - *Nostromo*
  - *Under Western Eyes*
  - *Typhoon*
  - *Victory*
  - *Youth*
  - *Secret Sharer*
  - *Heart of Darkness*
- COOPER, JAMES FENIMORE
  - *The Last of the Mohicans*
  - *The Deerslayer*
- CRANE, STEPHEN
  - *Open Boat*
  - *The Red Badge of Courage*
- CRICHTON, MICHAEL
  - *The Andromeda Strain*
  - *Congo*
  - *Jurassic Park*

- de BALZAC, HONORE
  - *Pere Goriot*
- DEFOE, DANIEL
  - *Robinson Crusoe*
  - *Moll Flanders*
- DICKENS, CHARLES
  - *David Copperfield*
  - *Great Expectations*
  - *Oliver Twist*
  - *Tale of Two Cities*
  - *Christmas Carol*
- DOSTOEVSKI, FYDOR
  - *Crime and Punishment*
- DOUGLAS, LLOYD
  - *The Robe*
- DOYLE, ARTHUR CONAN
  - *The Hound of the Baskervilles*
- DREISER, THEODORE
  - *The Great American Tragedy*
- DRURY, ALAN
  - *Advise and Consent*
- DUMAS, ALEXANDER
  - *The Count of Monte Cristo*
  - *The Three Musketeers*
- ELIOT, GEORGE
  - *Mill on the Floss*
  - *Adam Bede*
  - *Silas Marner*
- ELIOT, T.S.
  - *Murder in the Cathedral*
  - *The Cocktail Party*

- FAULKNER, WILLIAM
  - *The Bear*
  - *Intruder in the Dust*
  - *The Sound and the Fury*
  - *Fable*
- FERBER, EDNA
  - *Cimarron*
  - *Giant*
- FIELDING, HENRY
  - *Joseph Andrews*
  - *Tom Jones*
- FITZGERALD, F. SCOTT
  - *The Great Gatsby*
  - *Tender is the Night*
- FLAUBERT, GUSTAVE
  - *Madame Bovary*
- FORESTER, CECIL SCOTT
  - *Horatio Hornblower*
- FORSYTHE, FREDERICK
  - *The Odessa File*
- FRANK, PAT
  - *Alas Babylon*
- GALSWORTHY, JOHN
  - *The Forsyte Saga*
- GOLDING, WILLIAM
  - *The Lord of the Flies*
- GREENE, GRAHAM
  - *The Third Man*
  - *Heart of the Matter*
  - *Ministry of Fear*
  - *Our Man in Havana*
  - *Power and Glory*
  - *The Burnt Out Case*

- HARDY, THOMAS
    - *Jude the Obscure*
    - *Return of the Native*
    - *Tess of the D'Ubervilles*
    - *Mayor of Castrobridge*
- HAWTHORNE, NATHANIEL
    - *The Scarlet Letter*
    - *House of the Seven Gables*
- HEINLEIN, ROBERT
    - *Podkayne of Mars*
    - *Space Cadet*
- HEMMINGWAY, ERNEST
    - *Old Man and the Sea*
    - *Farewell to Arms*
    - *For Whom the Bell Tolls*
    - *The Sun Also Rises*
- HERSEY, JOHN
    - *A Bell for Adano*
- HILTON, JAMES
    - *Good-Bye Mr. Chips*
    - *Lost Horizon*
    - *Random Harvest*
- HOMER
    - *Illiad (w. Intro)*
    - *Odyssey (w. Intro)*
- HUDSON, WILLIAM H.
    - *Green Mansions*
- HUGO, VICTOR
    - *Les Miserables*
- HULME, KATHERINE
    - *The Nun's Story*
- HUXLEY, ALDOUS
    - *Brave New World*
    - *Point Counter Point*

- HYERDAL, THOR
  - *Kon-Tiki*
- JACKSON, HELEN
  - *Ramona*
- JAMES, HENRY
  - *The Ambassador*
  - *The American*
  - *Jenny*
  - *Miracle of the Bells*
- JOYCE, JAMES
  - *Portrait of an Artist*
- KESSEY, KEN
  - *One Flew Over the Cuckoo's Nest*
- KEYES, DANIEL
  - *Flowers for Algernon*
- KING, STEPHEN
  - *Fire Starter*
  - *Four Seasons*
  - plus others
- KIPLING, RUDYARD
  - *Captain Courageous*
  - *Jungle Book*
  - *Kim*
- KNEBER, F.
  - *Seven Days in May*
- KNOWLES, JOHN
  - *A Separate Peace*
- LEE, HARPER
  - *To Kill a Mockingbird*
- LEWIS, C.S.
  - *Out of a Silent Plant*
  - *Perelandra*
  - *That Hideous Strength*
  - *Until We Have Faces*
  - *Screwtape Letters*

- LEWIS, SINCLAIR
  - *Babbit*
  - *Main Street*
- LLEWELLYN, RICHARD
  - *How Green Was My Valley*
- LONDON, JACK
  - *All*
- MANN, THOMAS
  - *Magic Mountain*
- MARLOW, CHRISTOPHER
  - *Dr. Faustus*
- MAUGHAM, SOMERSET
  - *Of Human Bondage*
  - *The Moon and Sixpence*
- McCULLERS, CARSON
  - *Member of the Wedding*
  - *Ballad of the Sad Cafe*
- MELVILLE, HERMAN
  - *Moby Dick*
  - *Billy Bud*
- MICHENER, JAMES
  - *Centennial*
  - *Hawaii*
  - *Chesapeake*
  - plus others
- MILLER, ARTHUR
  - *Death of a Salesman*
  - *The Crucible*
- MITCHELL, MARGARET
  - *Gone With the Wind*
- MORE, THOMAS
  - *Utopia*
- NORDOFF/HALL
  - *Mutiny on the Bounty*

- O'CONNOR, FLANNERY
  - *The Last Hurrah*
- ORCZY, EMMUSKA
  - *The Scarlet Pimpernel*
- ORWELL, GEORGE
  - *Animal Farm*
  - *1984*
- PAGE, ELIZABETH
  - *The Tree of Liberty*
- PATON, ALAN
  - *Cry, the Beloved Country*
  - *Too Late the Phalarope*
- PLATH, SYLVIA
  - *The Bell Jar*
- POE, EDGAR ALLAN
  - *Tales and Poems*
- PORTER, KATHERINE ANN
  - *Flowering Judas*
  - *Pale Horse Pale Rider*
  - *Ship of Fools*
- RAND, AYN
  - *Anthym*
  - *The Fountainhead*
  - *Atlas Shrugged*
- REMARQUE, ERICH
  - *All Quiet on the Western Front*
  - *The Road Back*
- RICHTER, CONRAD
  - *The Sea of Grass*
- ROBERTS, KENNETH
  - *Northwest Passage*
- ROBINSON, HENRY
  - *The Cardinal*
- ROLVAAG, OLE
  - *Giants in the Earth*

- ROSTAND. EDMOND
  - *Cyrano De Bergerac*
- SALINGER, J.D.
  - *The Catcher in the Rye*
  - *Franny and Zooey*
- SAROYAN, WILLIAM
  - *The Human Comedy*
- SCOTT, WALTER
  - *Ivanhoe*
  - *The Talisman*
- SHAKESPEARE, WILLIAM
  - Any (not read as part of class requirement at school)
  - All plays
- SHAW, GEORGE BERNARD
  - *Pygmalian*
  - *Saint Joan*
- SHELLY, MARY
  - *Frankenstein*
- SHERIDAN, RICHARD
  - *The Rivals*
  - *School for Scandal*
- SHUTE, NEVIL
  - *On the Beach*
- SIENKIEWICZ, HENRI
  - *With Fire and Sword*
  - *Quo Vadis*
- SOPHOCLES
  - *Oedipus Rex*
  - *Antigone*
- ST. EXUPREY, ANTOINE
  - *The Little Prince*
  - *Night Flight*

- STEINBECK, JOHN
  - *Grapes of Wrath*
  - *The Pearl*
  - *Of Mice and Men*
  - *Travels with Charley*
  - *Tortilla Flats*
  - *Once There Was a War*
- STEVENSON, ROBERT LEWIS
  - *Kidnapped*
  - *Treasure Island*
  - *The Strange Case of Dr. Jekyll and Mr. Hyde*
- STOKER, BRAM
  - *Dracula*
- STONE, IRVING
  - *Lust for Life*
- STOWE, HARRIET B.
  - *Uncle Tom's Cabin*
- SWIFT, JONATHON
  - *Gulliver's Travels*
- THACKERAY, WILLIAM
  - *Vanity Fair*
- THOREAU, HENRY B.
  - *Walden*
- THURBER, JAMES
  - *My Life and Hard Times*
  - *Captain D.*
  - *The Thirteen Clocks*
  - *Thurber Carnival*
- TOLKIEN, J.R.R.
  - *The Hobbit*
  - *The Tolkien Trilogy*
- TOLSTOY, LEO
  - *War and Peace*
  - *Anna Karenina*

- TWAIN, MARK
  - *Huck Finn*
  - *Tom Sawyer*
  - *Life on the Mississippi*
- URIS, LEON
  - *Exodus*
  - *Mila 18*
  - *Trinity*
- VERNE, JULES
  - *20,000 Leagues Under the Sea*
  - plus others
- WALLACE, LEWIS
  - *Ben Hur*
- WARREN, ROBERT PENN
  - *All the King's Men*
- WAUGH, EVELYN
  - *The Loved One*
- WELLS, H.G.
  - *War of the Worlds*
- WILDER, THORNTON
  - *Bridge of San Louis Rey*
  - *Our Town*
- WOUK, HERMAN
  - *The Caine Mutiny*
  - *Marjorie Morningstar*
  - *The Winds of War*
  - *War and Remembrance*
- WYLIE, PHILIP
  - *When Worlds Collide*
  - *After Worlds Collide*

THE FOLLOWING AUTHORS CAN BE READ IN THEIR ENTIRETY OR IN EXCERPTS:

- ADAMS, HENRY
  - *The Education of Henry Adams*
- ANDERSON, SHERWOOD
  - *Winesburg, Ohio*
- AUGUSTINE, SAINT
  - *Confessions*
- BENNET, ARNOLD
  - *The Old Wives Tale*
- CARY, JOYCE
  - *Mister John*
- COLLINS, WILKIE
  - *The Moonstone*
- CONNELLY, MARK
  - *Green Pastures*
- DEWOHL, LOUIS
  - *The Quiet Light*
  - *The Restless Flame*
- GUARESCHI, GIOVANNI
  - *Little World of Dom Camillo*
- MARQUAND, J.
  - *Point of No Return*
- MERTON, THOMAS
  - *Seven Story Mountain*
- MORLEY, CHRISTOPHER
  - *The Haunted Bookshop*
- RUSKIN, JOHN
  - *Unto This Last*
- TARKINGTON, BOOTH
  - *The Magnificent Amberson*
  - *Monsieur Beaucaire*

BIOGRAPHIES

- ADAMS, HENRY
  - *Education of Henry Adams*
- ANDERSON MARIAN
  - *My Lord, What a Morning*
- ANTIN, MARY
  - *Promised Land*
- BARUCH, BARNARD M.
  - *Baruch: My Own Story*
- BELL, ERIC T.
  - *Men of Mathematics*
- BOSWELL, JAMES
  - *Life of Samuel Johnson*
- BOWEN, CATHERINE D.
  - *Yankee from Olympus: Justice Holmes and His Family*
- BUCK, PEARL S.
  - *My Several Worlds: A Personal Record*
- CASTELOT, ANDRE
  - *Queen of France*
- CELLINI, BENVENUTO
  - *Autobiography of Benvenuto Cellini*
- CHUTE, MARCHETTE
  - *Shakespeare of London*
- CLEMENS, SAMUEL L.
  - *Autobiography of Mark Twain*
- COUSINS, NORMAN
  - *Dr. Schweitzer of Lambarene*
- CUNLIFFE, MARCUS
  - *George Washington, Man and Monument*
- CURIE, EVE
  - *Madame Curie*

- DAVIS, BURKE
  - *They Called Him Stonewall*
- DeKRUIF, PAUL
  - *Microbe Hunters*
- FERGUSON, CHARLES W.
  - *Naked to Mine Enemies: The Life of Cardinal Wolsey*
- FERMI, LAURA
  - *Atoms in the Family*
- FORBES, ESTHER
  - *Paul Revere and the World He Lived In.*
- FRANK, ANNE
  - *Anne Frank: Diary of a Young Girl*
- FRANKLIN, BENJAMIN
  - *Benjamin Franklin; Autobiography*
- GREY, IAN
  - *Peter the Great: Emperor of All Russia*
- GUERARD, ALBERT LEON
  - *Napoleon I*
- HAGEDORN, HERMANN
  - *Roosevelt Family of Sagamore Hill*
- HART, MOSS
  - *Act One*
- HEISER, VICTOR
  - *American Doctor's Odyssey*
- JENKINS, ELIZABETH
  - *Elizabeth the Great*
- KELLER, HELEN
  - *Story of My Life*
- KELLY, AMY
  - *Eleanor of Aquitaine and the Four Kings*
- KENNEDY, JOHN F.
  - *Profiles in Courage*

- KRUTCH, JOSEPH WOOD
  - *Henry David Thoreau*
- LAMB, HAROLD
  - *Hannibal, One Man Against Rome*
- MAUROIS, ANDRE
  - *Ariel: The Life of Shelly*
- MERTON, THOMAS
  - *Seven Storey Mountain*
- MORISON, SAMUEL ELIOT
  - *Christopher Columbus, Mariner*
- PEPYS, SAMUEL
  - *Diary of Samuel Pepys*
- PLUTARCH
  - *Lives*
- ROOSEVELT, ELEANOR
  - *This I Remember*
- SANDBURG, CARL
  - *Always the Young Strangers*
  - *The Prairie Years and the War Years*
- ST. JOHN, ROBERT
  - *Ben Gurion*
- STEFFENS, LINCOLN
  - *Steffens Lincoln; Autobiography*
- STONE, IRVING
  - *Clarence Darrow for the Defense*
- STRACHEY, LYTTON
  - *Queen Victoria*
- STUART, JESSE
  - *Thread That Runs So True*
- TAYLOR, A.J.P.
  - *Bismarck*
- THARP, LOUISE HALL
  - *Peabody Sisters of Salem*

- VAN LOON, HENDRIK
  - *R.V.R.: The Life of Rembrandt van Rijn*
- VINING, ELIZABETH GRAY
  - *Windows for the Crown Prince*
- WASHINGTON, BOOKER T.
  - *Up From Slavery*
- WINWAR, FRANCES
  - *The Haunted Palace*
- WONG, JADE SNOW
  - *Fifth Chinese Daughter*
- WOOLF, VIRGINIA
  - *Flush: A Biography*
- YEVTUSHENKO, Yevegeny
  - *A Precocious Autobiography*

ACKNOWLEDGEMENTS

Grateful thanks go to Sharon Massey, Michael Angelo, Melissa Kelley, Christopher Ramirez, Kevin Angelo, Carrie Oprea and Tanya Wilson for their help and support in bringing this book to fruition.

Illustration by Bhavna Bhen.

RESOURCES

Baddeley, Alan D. *Essentials of Human Memory*. Hove, England: Psychology, 1999. Print.

Ebbinghaus, Hermann. *Memory: A Contribution to Experimental Psychology*. N.d. MS, Classics in the History of Psychology. Teachers College, Columbia University. *Classics in the History of Psychology*. York University, Toronto, Ontario. Web. 03 Oct. 2014. <http://psychclassics.yorku.ca/Ebbinghaus/index.htm>.

Schacter, Daniel L. *The Seven Sins of Memory: How the Mind Forgets and Remembers*. Boston: Houghton Mifflin, 2001. Print.

Made in the USA
Coppell, TX
15 September 2021

62439155R00055